IN OTHER WORDS
DEFINED

Acronyms defined by Words spoken to Self that will help Define and Affirm your own Self.

YSIDRA RIVERS © 2020

Table of Contents

Introduction 9

MAP #1 - AID – Attitude In Delivery 10

    MEANING 10

    APPLY 10

        PROVOCATION – YOUR TURN 12

            Exercise #1: Surround Yourself With Positivity 12

            Exercise #2: Challenge Your Inner Critic 14

            Exercise #3: Do Something For Someone Else 17

            Exercise #4: Take Time For Yourself/Self-care 18

            Exercise #5: Do One Thing That Scares You 19

MAP #2 - AMOS – A Moment Of Silence 21

    MEANING 21

    APPLY 21

        PROVOCATION – YOUR TURN 23

            Exercise #1: Sit In Silence 23

            Exercise #2: Practice Gratitude 25

            Exercise #3: One Day Of Silence 26

            Exercise #4: Find Your Body 27

MAP #3: ANT - A New Thought 29

    MEANING 29

IN OTHER WORDS DEFINED

    APPLY 29

    PROVOCATION – YOUR TURN 31

        Exercise #1 – Think Positive Thoughts 31

        Exercise #2 – The Mirror Technique 32

        Exercise #3 – Practice Gratitude 33

        Exercise #4 – Set Realistic Goals 34

        Exercise #5 – Release the Past 36

MAP #4: ATYP – According To Your Purpose 38

    MEANING 38

    APPLY 38

    PROVOCATION – YOUR TURN 40

        Exercise #1 – Make a Love List 40

        Exercise #2 – Write a Skills List 42

        Exercise #3 – Assess Your Personal History 42

        Exercise #4 – Take Advice 43

        Exercise #5 – Go On A Voyage Of Self Discovery 44

MAP #5: BFF – But Forgiveness First 51

    MEANING 51

    APPLY 51

    PROVOCATION – YOUR TURN 53

        Exercise #1 – Get Perspective 53

        Exercise #2 – Visualize Apology 56

        Exercise #3 – Roleplay Apology 57

        Exercise #4 – Write Forgiveness 60

MAP #6: BUY – Build Up Yourself 62

MEANING 62

APPLY 62

PROVOCATION – YOUR TURN 65

- Exercise #1 – Set Your Intentions 65
- Exercise #2 – Pay Daily Compliments 65
- Exercise #3 – Assess Your Self Talk 65
- Exercise #4 – Acknowledge Success 67

MAP #7: CYCLE - Challenge Your Current Limitations Eagerly 69

MEANING 69

APPLY 69

PROVOCATION – YOUR TURN 71

- Exercise #1 – Just Say Yes 71
- Exercise #2 – Challenge Yourself 72
- Exercise #3 – Power of Attorney 73
- Exercise #4 – Focus On Failure 73

MAP #8: ETC – Embracing The Change 80

MEANING 80

APPLY 80

PROVOCATION – YOUR TURN 81

- Exercise #1 – Cross Your Arms 81
- Exercise #2 – Change It Up 86
- Exercise #3 – Transformational Words 89
- Exercise #4 – As If 91

IN OTHER WORDS DEFINED

MAP #9: TRAVEL – Transforming Reality And Victoriously Exceeding Limits 94

    MEANING 94

    APPLY 94

    PROVOCATION – YOUR TURN 96

        Exercise #1 – Visualize the Next Level 96

        Exercise #2 – Eliminate Weakness 98

        Exercise #3 – Embrace Larger Challenges 99

        Exercise #4 – Push Your Limits 101

MAP #10: VACUUM – Vision And Creation Under Unusual Makings 103

    MEANING 103

    APPLY 103

    PROVOCATION – YOUR TURN 105

        Exercise #1 – Know Your Desires 105

        Exercise #2 – Know Your Why 106

        Exercise #3 – Know Your Schedule 107

        Exercise #4 – Protect the Schedule 108

MAP #11: WICH – Who's In Charge Here 110

    MEANING 110

    APPLY 110

    PROVOCATION - YOUR TURN 112

        Exercise #1 – Practice Confidence 112

        Exercise #2 – Stand Smarter 116

        Exercise #3 – Stretch Your Social Muscles 117

        Exercise #4 – Challenging Situations 119

MAP #12: WIDE – Write It Down Exactly 123

MEANING 123

APPLY 123

PROVOCATION - YOUR TURN 125

Exercise #1 – Be Specific 125

Exercise #2 – Make it Measurable 126

Exercise #3 – Keep Goals Attainable 127

Exercise #4 – Goals Should Be Relevant 130

Exercise #5 – Timebound 130

MAP #13: FILM – Faith In Live Motion 136

MEANING 136

APPLY 136

PROVOCATION – YOUR TURN 138

Exercise #1 – Affirmations 138

Exercise #2 – Gratitude Journal 138

Exercise #3 – Why Five Times 139

Exercise #4 – A Higher Version of Yourself 140

MAP #14: GRAPH – God Respects A Pure Heart 143

MEANING 143

APPLY 143

PROVOCATION - YOUR TURN 145

Exercise #1 – Identify Values 145

Exercise #2 – Work Values 152

Exercise #3 – Make an Action Plan 154

IN OTHER WORDS DEFINED

Exercise #4 – Cleaning up Your Language 155

MAP #15: No PMS – No Poverty Mind Sets 157

MEANING 157

APPLY 157

PROVOCATION – YOUR TURN 160

Exercise #1 – Mind Map 160

Exercise #2 – Challenge Your Current Mindset 160

Exercise #3 – Grow Your Grit 164

Exercise #4 – Grow Your Grit, Part 2 167

MAP #16: SYSTEM – Save Your Self To Escape Mediocre 172

MEANING 174

APPLY 174

PROVOCATION - YOUR TURN 176

Exercise #1 – Just Say Yes 176

Exercise #2 – Create a Snowball 178

Exercise #3 – Define Yourself 178

Exercise #4 – Enhancing Your Self Image 181

MAP #17: TEACH – Taking Empowerment Above Common Horizons 182

MEANING 184

APPLY 184

PROVOCATION - YOUR TURN 187

Exercise #1 – New Ideas 187

Exercise #2 – Self Assessment 188

Exercise #3 – Flex Your Assertiveness 189

IN OTHER WORDS DEFINED

    Exercise #4 – Empowerment Through Delegation 190

MAP #18: AFTER – Allowance For The Emergency Room 191

MEANING 191

APPLY 191

PROVOCATION – YOUR TURN 193

    Exercise #1 – Schedule 193

    Exercise #2 – Moisturize 193

    Exercise #3 – A Mini Meditation 194

    Exercise #4 – Journal to Relieve Stress 198

MAP #19: RARE – Releasing A Radical Expectancy 199

MEANING 201

APPLY 201

PROVOCATION – YOUR TURN 203

    Exercise #1 – Strengths & Weaknesses 203

    Exercise #2 – Self Reflective Questions 204

    Exercise #3 – Self Reflective Journal Prompts 216

    Exercise #4 – Write a Bucket List 216

MAP #20: BEG – Being Exceedingly Grateful 218

MEANING 218

APPLY 218

PROVOCATION – YOUR TURN 220

    Exercise #1 – Attitude for Gratitude 220

    Exercise #2 – Self Gratitude 221

    Exercise #3 – Social Gratitude 221

Exercise #4 – The One Thing 222

MAP #21: BIOS – Belief In One's Self 224

MEANING 224

APPLY 224

PROVOCATION – YOUR TURN 226

Exercise #1 – Love Yourself 226

Exercise #2 – I Have Skills 226

Exercise #3 – I Can Achieve 227

Exercise #4 – I Can Overcome 228

Exercise #5 – I Can Help 228

MAP #22: BOWS – Be Okay With Silence 229

MEANING 229

APPLY 229

PROVOCATION – YOUR TURN 231

Exercise #1 – Inhale, Exhale Colors 231

Exercise #2 – The Body Scan 231

Exercise #3 – Breathing Hands 233

Exercise #4 – In The Still of the Night 235

Introduction

In Other Words Defined are affirmations that I've created to speak intentionally and directly into myself, as I looked in the mirror. Although prior to this habit, I've never carried a mirror, however, today I make it a point to for this purpose. Because of my learning style, using acronyms made them easier for me to remember.

Each acronym is defined, using other words, hence, In Other Words Defined. Each word was created to affirm what I knew, however, I was not experiencing. Making these affirmations to myself, while looking at myself 2 or 3 times a day helped me with my coping skills, confidence and it has strengthened my faith in God.

By me affirming these empowering affirmations to myself, I found myself sharing them with others and challenging them to also look themselves in the mirror and affirm the same into the eyes that was looking back at them.

As Dr. Tracey J. Johnson says, to the degree of which you experience a thing, will be the same degree to which you will express it. I pray that each word you speak into yourself will not only be affirmed to yourself by yourself, however, may they also be expressed effortlessly.

Ysidra
dare2cthedifference.com

MAP #1
AID – Attitude In Delivery

MEANING
AID – Attitude In Delivery
My work is enjoyable and fulfilling

"The good news is that the bad news can be turned into good news when you change your attitude" - Robert H. Schuller

APPLY

Attitude In Delivery is important because our attitude is the very thing that creates the environment, we find ourselves in any given situation. Our attitude establishes the energy, flow and direction of things. Our attitude is also key when it comes to how receptive the people, we interact with will be, including those we are speaking

to, sharing with or selling to. It is our attitude that greatly determines whether they will be open to and receptive to what we convey.

Our attitude has the power to change the attitude and minds of others. Our attitude has the power to control our environment. When our attitude is confident, pleasant, and joyous, the people around us become much more receptive and our messages are likely to be clear and well received.

Being well received is a key component for our communication goals, in both our personal and professional lives.

If we do not convey confidence and strength and if our message is not solid and delivered with positive intent, how can we expect to be well received by our audience?

To this end, self-confidence benefits you in many ways, it is a key attitude for success. Self-confidence allows you to manage your fears, promotes a positive mental attitude and promotes success. That confidence elevates your attitude and in turn elevates the message you convey to others. Confident people hold their heads high and their positivity shines through the messages they deliver.

Attitude In Delivery! Today you are delivering yourself. Be sure to have an attitude that is worth Cash On Delivery and not Return To Sender!

 **PROVOCATION – YOUR TURN**

Exercise #1: Surround Yourself With Positivity

To build a positive mindset surround yourself with positive people. **List 5 people in your life that are positive thinkers/optimists**

_____
_____
_____
_____
_____

Make a plan on how you will spend more time with these people and learn from their influence

_____
_____
_____
_____
_____
_____
_____
_____
_____
_____

Exercise #2: Challenge Your Inner Critic

Our inner voice has a lot do with our confidence level. When that voice is negative and self-defeating, it affects our confidence. It's time to challenge that inner critic and change the messages.

For the next 7 days write down in the left column every negative thing your inner critic tells you for example, "why can't you be more efficient like Joan?" or "your lips are too big" or "why can't you do anything right" **and in the right column counter that thought with a positive self-supporting statement,** for example, "you are an individual and that makes you special" "you are beautiful in body and soul," I am good at my job, I am a great mom, I am a great friend" etc.…

Keep adding to this list as your inner critic speaks to you and check it often focusing on the counter positive message and repeating that to yourself instead of the negative.

NEGATIVE THOUGHTMESSAGE	COUNTER POSITIVE THOUGHTMESSAGE
MONDAY	

IN OTHER WORDS DEFINED

TUESDAY	

WEDNESDAY	

THURSDAY	

By **YSIDRA RIVERS**

IN OTHER WORDS DEFINED

FRIDAY

SATURDAY

SUNDAY

Exercise #3: Do Something For Someone Else

"You get what you give." If you act in positivity, you reap positivity and you feel positive.

Plan 5 things you will do for someone else. Repeat as often as possible. Ideas include pay someone a compliment, buy someone a meal, donate your time to a good cause, show your gratitude to someone in your life, call someone you care about and tell them why you appreciate them.

_____
_____
_____
_____
_____
_____
_____
_____
_____
_____
_____
_____
_____
_____
_____
_____
_____
_____
_____
_____

Exercise #4: Take Time For Yourself/Self-care

Self-care is key in promoting healthy self-esteem and self-esteem is key to building self-confidence, and positivity about and within yourself and the world.

List 10 things you can do just for yourself that show you that you care about you. For example, get a massage, treat yourself to date night with yourself, reward yourself for something you achieved, do one thing to improve your diet, take a mental health day and just relax, take a spa day, unplug for 1 hour while you sit on grass and enjoy nature.

1. _____
   _____

2. _____
   _____

3. _____
   _____

4. _____
   _____

5. _____
   _____

6. _____
   _____

7. _____
   _____

8. _____
   _____

9. _____
   _____

10. _____
    _____

Exercise #5: Do One Thing That Scares You

This exercise helps you build confidence. For the next 7 days do one thing that scares you. Keep repeating until you start to feel your confidence build. Feel the fear but do it anyway. This can be anything from confronting someone about a wrong, apologizing to someone, sleeping without a night light or even just starting a conversation with a stranger.

List those things that scare you here and then reflect on how you felt once you did them.

_____
_____
_____
_____
_____
_____
_____
_____

IN OTHER WORDS > DEFINED

MAP #2
AMOS – A Moment Of Silence

MEANING
AMOS – A Moment Of Silence
Meditation is integral to my daily routine

"The greatest battles of life are fought out daily in the silent chambers of the soul" - David O. McKay

APPLY

Scripture tells us that we ought to meditate, study, pray, and think things out. A Moment of Silence helps us to realign ourselves, clear our minds and detox mental impurities.

A lot of advertisement wrestles for our attention. The tech age brings a lot of mental noise. TV, computers, cell phones and billboards peppered all over our streets are all sending messages, many of which we have become immune to and so we have no conscious awareness of them. There are even subliminal messages strategically sent to us, without our permission or our awareness.

A Moment of Silence is vital to our financial, spiritual, physical, emotional, social and mental wellbeing. Did you know that there is a seed in every living thing and anything without a seed cannot naturally reproduce?

IN OTHER WORDS — DEFINED

It is in that Moment of Silence when we reach that seed, and when it can be developed, nurtured and strengthened. Away from the noise and energy of the outside world. And, most importantly, away from the control of anything and anyone outside of ourselves.

Mothers of past used to say you need to spend more time in the closet. In the closet is where it is just you, yourself and God.

In silence we find one of the greatest gifts God offers us. It is the time we renew and strengthen our truest inner selves. In silence we find real joy and enlightenment.

In silence, we open our souls to grace, awareness and gratitude. In silence we find compassion, not only for ourselves, but also for others and the world.

By **YSIDRA RIVERS**

In silence we become aware of being human. We get in touch with how we and life are so vulnerable, and we see clearly our own humility while letting go of self-importance and reaffirming our respect for life.

In silence we become keenly aware of our bare and naked self. Just being. At peace. Grounded. At rest. Centered. Aware of our self just as the self without relation to our roles in life, such as those related to work, family and day to day life. In silence we can just be, in peace, and present in the moment, completely separate of what we do, worry about or wish for.

Sitting in silence teaches us patience. In silence we find the will, desire and capability to let go. We stop reacting and start receiving.

In silence we hear more than we ever do in a noisy world. Within a highly elevated sense of awareness we can hear our deepest thoughts, desires and messages from our true self, which bring the highest level of enlightenment.

There's a seed inside of you! In silence you can have a breakthrough!

PROVOCATION – YOUR TURN

Exercise #1: Sit In Silence

Find a quiet place and a comfortable place to sit. It's your choice where, outside, inside, on the couch or on the grass, just be sure that your spine is straight. Turn off your phone, and all noise sources.

IN OTHER WORDS DEFINED

Sit in silence for 10 minutes. Let your mind just be. Focus on your breathing, keep it steady. Inhale to the count of 5 and then exhale to the count of 5. Focus on your body, envision all your body parts as you sit there in silence. When your mind gets antsy and thoughts start to stream in, refocus to your breath. When you feel like you can't take it, refocus on your breath. You will feel uncomfortable, and that's ok, this is not easy to do in the beginning, but it will get easier with practice. Meditation or sitting in silence is a practice that takes time to perfect and get comfortable with. **Repeat this exercise daily, or at least twice a week. As you get better add more time.**

Note how you felt and any revelations you had during your 10 minutes of silence:

_____
_____
_____
_____
_____
_____
_____
_____
_____
_____
_____
_____
_____
_____
_____
_____
_____
_____
_____
_____
_____

Exercise #2: Practice Gratitude

Gratitude is one of the best ways to get in touch with our inner self. It grounds us and keeps us centered, and that is an integral part of learning to revel in silence.

List 10 things/people you are grateful for right now. It can be anything from your morning cup of coffee to your children. Be specific. Feel the gratitude. Imagine what life would be like without these things. We take a lot for granted, for example, have you ever had an electrical outage at your home? Once this occurs you realize how much you take modern conveniences for granted.

1. _____

2. _____

IN OTHER WORDS ▸ DEFINED

3. _____

4. _____

5. _____

6. _____

7. _____

8. _____

9. _____

10. _____

Exercise #3: One Day Of Silence

Be silent for 24 hours. Pick any day and don't say a single word. More than likely you will absolutely have to speak at some point during the day, even if it is just a few words. Go ahead but return to silence immediately after. Take a few minutes to reflect on what you said, and what motivated you to say it.

IN OTHER WORDS — DEFINED

Once you complete this exercise, reflect on it here. How was it? How did it feel? What went through your mind? What were the difficulties? What did you discover? What gifts did you find in the silence?

_____
_____
_____
_____
_____
_____
_____
_____
_____
_____
_____
_____
_____
_____
_____
_____
_____
_____
_____
_____
_____
_____
_____
_____
_____

_____
_____
_____
_____
_____
_____

Exercise #4: Find Your Body

Take a few minutes to focus on your body. Repeat this daily if possible or at least 3 times a week. Sit in a quiet place. Start with your head and go all the way to your feet, focus on one body part at a time. Don't forget your hair, eye lashes, eye brows, stomach, inside and out. Dig deep. Use all your senses, sight, smell, sound and touch.

Consider:

How does this part feel?

How does this part look?

How does this part serve me?

What does this part do?

Why am I grateful for this part?

Can this part use some work?

Do I neglect this part?

MAP #3:
ANT - A New Thought

 **MEANING**

ANT – A New Thought
I choose thoughts that nourish and support me

*"Self-discipline begins with the mastery of your thoughts.
If you don't control what you think, you can't control what you do."*
- Napoleon Hill

 **APPLY**

We have full power over our thoughts. To create thoughts. To change thoughts. To believe or not believe thoughts. To choose thoughts. Be it unto you as you believe! When I was a child, I thought as a child...this helps me understand and remember that I have the power to create and it all starts with A New Thought.

Graham Cooke always says, "If you don't like the thoughts you're thinking, think new thoughts."

A New Thought can change any situation around! A New thought can change your life!

A New Thought can change who you are and what you do. A New Thought makes all things possible.

IN OTHER WORDS > DEFINED

We have the power to create something new, and it all starts with A Thought. Sometimes we forget how much power we have. We allow our thoughts to control our behavior, even when those thoughts are unsettling and self-defeating. We entertain and dwell in thoughts that arrest our emotions or are ungodly, unhealthy and out of control.

We must remember that thoughts are not reality. Thoughts do not have to control us. We can change our thoughts and create new thoughts that support our emotional and mental wellbeing. In turn those new positive self-supporting thoughts will change our behaviors, because it is our thinking and mindset that dictate how we act.

Interrupt that energy zapping, non-empowering thought and replace it with A New Thought. Consider ants, they have the ability to carry things up to one hundred times their weight, they're big thinkers and great planners.

By **YSIDRA RIVERS**

A New Thought…. everything starts with a thought. If you don't like your thoughts, think up some new ones, you are in control.

 ## PROVOCATION – YOUR TURN

Exercise #1 – Think Positive Thoughts

It can be difficult to maintain a positive thought process when you're lost in an old way of thinking. Start making changes by learning how to intentionally think positive thoughts.

You can start by thinking of five amazing things that are going on in your life right now.

1. _____
   _____

2. _____
   _____

3. _____
   _____

4. _____
   _____

5. _____
   _____

Now, build a series of positive affirmations around the five things you listed above!

_____
_____
_____
_____
_____
_____
_____
_____
_____
_____
_____
_____
_____
_____
_____
_____
_____

Practice these as often as possible, from the time you wake up in the morning until you slip off to sleep at night.

Exercise #2 – The Mirror Technique

Are you familiar with the mirror technique? It's really simple. **Position yourself in front of a mirror and look yourself in the eye as you list all of your positive traits.** You should do this first thing in the morning and again before bed. In the space below, make a note of some of the most surprising traits you listed. You might be surprised how many positive aspects of yourself you come up with.

_____

Exercise #3 – Practice Gratitude

What better way to change your thoughts than through practicing gratitude.

Make a list of five people in your life that you appreciate.

1. _____
2. _____
3. _____
4. _____
5. _____

Now, name five things in your life you are grateful for.

1. _____
2. _____
3. _____
4. _____
5. _____

Now, list five activities, things or hobbies you regularly practice and love.

1. _____
2. _____
3. _____
4. _____
5. _____

You have a lot to be grateful for, don't you?

Exercise #4 – Set Realistic Goals

It can be difficult to remain positive and think good thoughts when you set yourself up to fail. If you believe in the power of goal setting, it's time to get realistic. Your goals should stretch you, yes, but they should be achievable. It's time to get real and set realistic goals. **Below, create a goal for this week. It should be something that is specific, measurable, and achievable.**

IN OTHER WORDS > DEFINED

Weekly Goal

_____
_____
_____
_____
_____
_____
_____
_____
_____
_____
_____
_____
_____

Don't stop there, set a monthly goal following the same pattern.

Monthly Goal

_____
_____
_____
_____
_____
_____
_____
_____
_____
_____

_____
_____
_____
_____
_____
_____
_____
_____

Now, go out there and get it!

Exercise #5 – Release the Past

To create a new thought, you have to let go of old thoughts. This is something we can do by discovering past pain that lingers.

In the left hand column you can make a note of the issue from your past you continue to deal with. In the right hand column, it's time to get honest. Often, we hold onto these issues from our past because we can't take responsibility for them. We hold on because we blame someone else. So, be honest with yourself and make a note of who you hold responsible for this issue. If it is you, then write your own name in the box.

THE ISSUE	THE BLAME

IN OTHER WORDS — DEFINED

Now what? Now it's time to forgive, let it go, and move on! It's time to change your thought process and create a new thought.

MAP #4:
ATYP – According To Your Purpose

MEANING
ATYP – According To Your Purpose
I live life according to my values

*"The greatest tragedy in life is not death,
but a life without a purpose." - MYLES MONROE*

APPLY

The primary definitions of the word purpose…

/noun/ "the reason for which something exists or is done, made or used."

/verb/ "to set as an intention or goal for oneself"

To be "purpose driven" means having a passion and a drive for something that we find profoundly important. The pursuit of passion.

Our life purpose motivates us to get out of bed in the morning. It is the one thing that more than anything guides our decisions, shapes our goals, influences our behaviors, and most importantly, create profound meaning in our lives.

IN OTHER WORDS DEFINED

Those who have purpose in life are the most satisfied with their lives, no matter if they are rich, no matter if they are lacking, no matter what. It is the foundation of true happiness.

You were born with your own personality and your strengths were recognized by your parents before you knew how to walk. You have a purpose. You were born for a specific reason.

There will be a longing in the very essence of all that you are, until you fulfill your purpose. You will hear words, have visions, experience clear thoughts and receive unearthly ideas that will ultimately drive you, lead you, draw you and/or even provoke you in a direction that no man, woman or beast has ever traveled – your personal purpose.

There is one life ready to be changed so it could live fulfilled, satisfied and awed from the higher state of within. It' only ATYP!

By **YSIDRA RIVERS**

It's According To Your Purpose that you will do some things effortlessly. It's According To Your Purpose that certain people and things will be attracted to you and you will be attracted to them.

 **PROVOCATION – YOUR TURN**

Determining your purpose in life can be a challenge. These exercises will help.

Exercise #1 – Make a Love List

What do you love? Make a list of the things you really enjoy doing. This will be your love list and you should be honest, outrageous, creative, and open minded as you create this list. Just let it all out – everything you love to do.

_____
_____
_____
_____
_____
_____
_____
_____
_____
_____
_____
_____
_____
_____
_____

IN OTHER WORDS > DEFINED

Exercise #2 – Write a Skills List

While your passion may be your true purpose, it's important to know what you're good at. So, use this opportunity to make a list of all of your skills. **What are you great at? What can you do with ease?**

_____
_____
_____
_____
_____
_____
_____
_____
_____
_____
_____
_____
_____
_____
_____
_____
_____
_____
_____
_____
_____
_____
_____
_____
_____

Exercise #3 – Assess Your Personal History

In the life you have lived thus far, you have faced unique challenges. What are some of the obstacles you have faced and overcome in your life? Look at your personal history and think about what you've conquered. **What skills or traits do these challenges highlight for you, what can you share with the world?**

_____
_____
_____
_____
_____
_____
_____
_____
_____
_____
_____
_____
_____
_____
_____
_____
_____
_____
_____
_____
_____
_____
_____
_____

Exercise #4 – Take Advice

You may need to phone a friend (or family member). Sometimes objectivity is necessary. **Ask others about skills, traits, and strengths you may have missed. Reach out to colleagues as well, this will give you a wide range of traits to go on.**

_____
_____
_____
_____
_____
_____
_____
_____
_____
_____
_____
_____
_____
_____
_____
_____
_____
_____
_____
_____
_____
_____
_____
_____
_____

Exercise #5 – Go On A Voyage Of Self Discovery

Now, it's time to process the above and push further by asking yourself questions that will facilitate your self-discovery. **What would you do happily without a paycheck?**

_____
_____
_____
_____
_____
_____
_____
_____
_____
_____
_____
_____
_____
_____
_____
_____
_____
_____
_____
_____
_____
_____
_____
_____
_____

IN OTHER WORDS — DEFINED

What do people tell you to do more of?

IN OTHER WORDS DEFINED

What would you like to accomplish or experience before you retire?

_____
_____
_____
_____
_____
_____
_____
_____
_____
_____
_____
_____
_____
_____
_____
_____
_____
_____
_____
_____
_____
_____

How would you spend your days if you were filthy rich?

_____
_____
_____
_____

IN OTHER WORDS DEFINED

Describe the details of your perfect day.

What sets your soul alight?

IN OTHER WORDS > DEFINED

MAP #5:
BFF – But Forgiveness First

 **MEANING**
BFF – But Forgiveness First
I look at others' wrongdoings through forgiving eyes

"Forgiveness does not change the past but it does enlarge the future."
- Paul Lewis Boese

"Forgive others not because they deserve forgiveness but because you deserve peace." *- Johnathan Lockwood Huie*

 **APPLY**

Has someone ever wronged you? Odds are they have. Maybe they wronged you so terribly that you hold onto that resentment years down the road. Every now and then you remember this person who wronged you and you dream of revenge or just indulge yourself in hating them.

Holding a grudge actually causes your mind and body stress. It's like making a poison for someone else but drinking it yourself. All that time you spend stalking this person on social media, longing for them to come across bad times is time you could've spent planning and actually living your own life. Or maybe the person is still in your life and you have to see and hate them every day. That's a lot of energy to spend.

This treatment makes the person into a star obsession in your life. They have already done enough to you; they don't need to divert your precious time and efforts away from your goals and toward hating them. It isn't fair to you and they don't deserve such recognition.

Maybe you dream of revenge. Maybe one day you get this person back in a poetic way that all goes according to plan. Will this get you a better life? Will the pleasure last? Will this person then strike you back and cause a war of revenge?

If you cannot forgive others, you may start guarding yourself and keeping people at arm's length. This is a lonely lifestyle and one that is often a self-fulfilling prophecy. People will see you as petty and you will see them as evil.

Through all this you are giving away your power.

Forgive this person, even if they are not sorry. Until you do, they will have power over you and some of them might even enjoy this fact. Forgive. Forgive those who wrong you and take a breath of fresh air. Forgiveness is for you, not for them. Forgive so you can be free.

 **PROVOCATION – YOUR TURN**

Exercise #1 – Get Perspective

One of the most effective ways to extend forgiveness is by putting yourself in someone else's shoes. Let's try this below. **Pressures. What pressure could the person have been under to make them behave the way they did?**

_____
_____
_____
_____
_____
_____
_____
_____
_____
_____
_____
_____
_____

Past. What background or underlying factors could have contributed to this person's behavior?

IN OTHER WORDS DEFINED

Personality. What events may have helped forge this person's personality?

Provocations. Did you do anything to provoke the behavior? If you struggle to think of something, was there something the person could have perceived as a provocation?

Plans. Did this person have good intentions? Were they trying to help or correct you, but did it poorly?

_____
_____
_____
_____
_____
_____
_____
_____
_____
_____
_____
_____
_____
_____
_____
_____
_____
_____
_____
_____
_____
_____
_____
_____
_____
_____
_____
_____
_____

Exercise #2 – Visualize Apology

You may have an easier time extending forgiveness if you visualize or fantasize about the apology itself. Imagine the person offering you a genuine apology and showing remorse for their behavior. It doesn't matter if it's true, it doesn't matter if you never have a face to face meeting with the person. Just visualize it. You can forgive them now. **If you are still struggling to let go, use the space below to detail why that is and what you can do to get there.**

_____
_____
_____
_____
_____
_____
_____
_____
_____
_____
_____
_____
_____
_____
_____
_____
_____
_____
_____
_____

Exercise #3 – Roleplay Apology

If visualization isn't working, then you can try a roleplay scenario. Get someone to stand in for the offender in question and work through the issue. Ask them why they did what they did, ask about the emotions they felt or, whatever else you feel you need to know before you can fully let it go. **This exercise is all about getting a grip on the big picture that may have created the problem. Essentially, you're trying to give the offender the benefit of the doubt. Your ability to extend empathy does not mean you are simply excusing poor behavior. It's about releasing anger and hurt you're holding onto. It's holding you back.**

How did you feel during the roleplay? What emotions did you experience during the questioning period and at the point of forgiveness?

IN OTHER WORDS DEFINED

Exercise #4 – Write Forgiveness

Now is the time to let it all out and let it go by writing a letter of forgiveness to the person who harmed you. Talk about how their behavior impacted you, how you felt, what you wished would have happened, and close with forgiveness and empathy. You don't have to send this letter.

_____
_____
_____
_____
_____
_____
_____
_____
_____
_____
_____
_____
_____
_____
_____
_____
_____
_____
_____
_____
_____
_____
_____
_____
_____

IN OTHER WORDS DEFINED

MAP #6:
BUY – Build Up Yourself

M **MEANING**
BUY – Build Up Yourself
I am beautiful inside and out

"Love yourself. It is important to stay positive because beauty comes from the inside out." - Jenn Proske

A **APPLY**

Build Up Yourself, for there will be moments, times and even days when we won't be able to find a cheer leader, friend or confidant anywhere. There will be many a times, in our lives, when not one individual can be found when we believe that we need them most.

I believe in those times when no one can be found, are times when definitely, positively, absolutely, times when God is getting our attention. Those are times when we need God and God wants us.

Warren Buffet says investing in yourself supersedes all other investments. Teach yourself new things, take care of yourself, and build yourself up. Building yourself up does not only mean that you repeat self-care mantras and pat yourself on the back. It means that you take quality care of yourself and, when it's time, you push yourself on to better things.

IN OTHER WORDS DEFINED

Too many people think that self-care is a bath or a ten dollar milk shake. These short term rewards, while sometimes helpful, can lead to a lifestyle that avoids your real problems and sticks you in a rut. Sometimes self-care is hard. You need to eat the right foods and schedule sleep to have energy. You need to take proper care of your hygiene. You need to schedule doctor and mental health appointments that you actually go to. Then, maybe once you are doing better at a few of those things, go ahead and get that milkshake on the way home.

Build Up Yourself. I am a firm believer that the deposits which we make within ourselves, stretch much further than the deposits that others make into us. Tell yourself, with every form of expression and communications that you can possibly speak. Tell yourself with your mouth, with your face, with your body, with your mind and with your heart…. "I AM NEVER TOO LOW THAT I CAN NOT BE BUILT UP" "THERE IS NO BETTER OR GREATER PERSON TO BUILD ME UP THAN ME"

By **YSIDRA RIVERS**

IN OTHER WORDS DEFINED

To build something there is a substance you must use. Build, raise up, lift up, elevate. To build yourself, there is an essence of yourself that you must know. This takes time to cultivate, manipulate and from within yourself of yourself demonstrate. What must you know? You must know how to reach yourself. You must know what makes you low. You must know when you're open to yourself. Most importantly, you must know there is an essence that is separate from you.

Build Up Yourself, for there will be moments, times and even days when we won't be able to find a cheer leader, friend or confidant anywhere. There will be many a times, in our lives, when not one individual can be found when we believe that we need them most.

I believe in those times when no one can be found, are times when definitely, positively, absolutely, times when God is getting our attention. Those are times when we need God and God wants us.

Build Up Yourself. I am a firm believer that the deposits which we make within ourselves, stretch much further than the deposits that others make into us. Tell yourself, with every form of expression and communications that you can possibly speak. Tell yourself with your mouth, with your face, with your body, with your mind and with your heart…."I AM NEVER TOO LOW THAT I CAN NOT BE BUILT UP" THERE IS NO BETTER OR GREATER PERSON TO BUILD ME UP THAN ME"

To build something there is a substance you must use. Build, raise up, lift up, elevate. To build yourself, there is an essence of yourself that you must know. This takes time to cultivate, manipulate and from within yourself of yourself demonstrate. What must you know? You must know how to reach yourself. You must know what makes you low. You must know when you're open to yourself. Most important, you must know there is an essence that is separate from you.

By **YSIDRA RIVERS**

 PROVOCATION – YOUR TURN

Exercise #1 – Set Your Intentions

Start every day with the intention that it's going to be a great day! This is a method to train your mind to automatically think positively. In turn, it will make it easier for you to build yourself up! While we easily forget our good memories, we seem to find it easy to hold onto the bad ones. **In the space below, make a note of the good things you experienced yesterday and the goodness you expect to see today.**

_____
_____
_____

Exercise #2 – Pay Daily Compliments

At the end of every day, write out a compliment to yourself and pop it in a jar. This is the bare minimum, *at least* one a day. You can complement yourself as often as you like. Choose a period of time to pass before you open the jar and read out all of the compliments you have paid yourself. You can make it a birthday present to yourself, do it quarterly or on New Year's Day. It's up to you.

Exercise #3 – Assess Your Self Talk

An important part of building yourself up is being aware of how you speak to yourself. If you are constantly negative, if you constantly beat yourself up, then you're actively tearing yourself down. To build yourself up, you need to practice positive self-talk. Be kind, be positive, and treat yourself with empathy. **In the space**

below, make a list of positive statements you can use to encourage positive self-talk.

_____
_____
_____
_____
_____
_____
_____
_____
_____
_____
_____
_____
_____
_____
_____
_____
_____
_____
_____
_____
_____
_____
_____
_____
_____
_____
_____
_____
_____
_____

Exercise #4 – Acknowledge Success

Don't downplay your success, acknowledge it, and celebrate it to build yourself up! Don't brush it off as no big deal or something anyone can do. It might be true, but everyone didn't do it, you did it. **Make a list of some of your greatest successes and pat yourself on the back!**

_____
_____
_____
_____
_____
_____
_____
_____
_____
_____
_____
_____
_____
_____
_____
_____
_____
_____
_____
_____
_____
_____
_____
_____

IN OTHER WORDS ► DEFINED

By **YSIDRA RIVERS**

MAP #7:
CYCLE - Challenge Your Current Limitations Eagerly

MEANING
CYCLE – Challenge Your Current Limitations Eagerly
My success is my responsibility

"The only real limitations on your abilities is the level of your desires. If you want it badly enough there are no limits on what you can achieve."
- Brian Tracy

APPLY

CYCLE! When I think about cycles, I think about old cycles. I think about cycles that run automatically. Cycles that need to be broken. For me, these are key associations for cycles.

Maybe it's a mindset CYCLE. Maybe it's a habit CYCLE. Maybe it's an area that I lack discipline CYCLE. No matter what it is, I perceive it to be positive….an opportunity to grow (as painful as it may be). The anticipation and expectancy of this CYCLE being broken is exciting, and I look forward to it.

What CYCLE comes to your mind that you need to end, break and/or remove, in your life?

IN OTHER WORDS > DEFINED

Challenge Your Current Limitations Eagerly! To challenge something takes courage. To challenge something takes effort, intentionality, determination, and tenacity. To challenge means it's not going to be easy.

This exercise is vital because when we begin to challenge anything that limits us, and we do it with the proper attitude, it means that our willingness and abilities are greater than our limitations.

When we have defeated that perception of limitation, we realize that it was all an illusion, a misfire of our perception because the only limitations that will ever exist are those we place on ourselves.

If we embrace a limitless mindset, the possibilities become unlimited. Everything becomes possible, and we become invincible in our pursuits.

By **YSIDRA RIVERS**

PROVOCATION – YOUR TURN

Exercise #1 – Just Say Yes

While we encourage you to say no more in general to the things that are draining your energy, today, we encourage you to just say yes! (This doesn't mean to say yes to working late or taking on someone else's workload.), **Say yes to calling in because you're feeling well, say yes to meeting your friend for lunch, just say yes to opportunities you would normally shy away from or adventures you would run from. Use the space below to discuss how you felt by challenging your limitations.**

_____
_____
_____
_____
_____
_____
_____
_____
_____
_____
_____
_____
_____
_____
_____
_____
_____

IN OTHER WORDS | **DEFINED**

_____
_____
_____
_____
_____
_____
_____
_____
_____
_____
_____

Exercise #2 – Challenge Yourself

Set yourself a series of challenges that push you outside of your limitations. Some examples of the challenges you can set: Asking for the promotion you deserve, making eye contact and smiling at strangers, say more than *fine* when someone asks how you are, speak up when the meal you ordered isn't right.

THE TRIGGER	THE CHALLENGE

Exercise #3 – Power of Attorney

If you consistently struggle to push beyond your limitations, then hand over the control to someone else. If you know an adventurer, if you know a planner, an adrenaline junkie, then now is the time to give them a call. **Allow them to plan your day (or week). Let them set your challenges and throw yourself into it. How did it feel to let go of control? How did it feel to step outside of your comfort zone and challenge your limitations so aggressively?**

_____
_____
_____
_____
_____

IN OTHER WORDS > DEFINED

By **YSIDRA RIVERS**

Exercise #4 – Focus On Failure

One of the biggest reasons we struggle with our limitations is a fear of failure. Let's focus on failure. **In the space below, write about a time you failed, how it felt and how you recovered.**

IN OTHER WORDS > DEFINED

IN OTHER WORDS **DEFINED**

Now, visualize yourself in this situation again and navigate the scenario with the lessons you have learned. How did it turn out?

IN OTHER WORDS DEFINED

By **YSIDRA RIVERS**

IN OTHER WORDS DEFINED

If you recognize the lesson in failure, why would you allow fear to hold you back now? Challenge your limitations!

MAP #8:
ETC – Embracing The Change

 **MEANING**
ETC – Embracing The Change
I embrace opportunities that can make a positive change in my life

"Just when the caterpillar thought the world was over, it became a butterfly."
- proverb

"Change is hardest at the beginning/ Messiest in the middle/ And best at the end" - Robin Sharma

 **APPLY**

Embracing the Change! Change is inevitable. Change is coming and change is going. Rather we are prepared, willing or expecting it. Growth, knowledge, experience, joy and love. All of those things bring about a change.

Life itself, with each new day, brings about a change. Each day brings about something, someone, some ways, some thoughts, new. Embrace the Change!

When we resists that which is sure then we hinder our own growth. We limit that which we can, we believe, we hope to and/or even desire to obtain or receive. We cause havoc, disorder and uneasiness in our environment, when we resist change.

Have you ever witness a person drowning before? For those who are not trained as life guards, it is always recommended to allow the person that is drowning to lose consciousness first, before jumping in to save them. This is recommended because the strength of the person drowning can overtake the person trying to help.

This is what takes place when we do not embrace the change. It is as if we're going against the grain. As if we are denying what really is. As if we are resisting what is meant to be. When we stop fighting and stop resisting the unknown and start trusting that the change will not hurt us but make things bigger, better and brighter for us, we can and live, work and play with ease.

We must embrace the change and allow that change to embrace us.

PROVOCATION – YOUR TURN

Exercise #1 – Cross Your Arms

Cross (or fold) your arms. Imagine you are bored, sitting on a bench waiting for someone or you are feeling defensive. Now that you have done that, fold your

arms the other way. Just reverse your position. It's not easy, is it? We fold our arms naturally, it's something we do automatically. So, the idea of doing it in a different way is challenging.

How did it feel?

_____
_____
_____
_____
_____
_____
_____
_____
_____
_____
_____
_____
_____
_____
_____
_____
_____
_____
_____
_____
_____
_____
_____
_____
_____

Did you have to think about it, or did you naturally flip your position?

Did you feel comfortable even though it was different?

What makes you resistant to change?

IN OTHER WORDS DEFINED

How can you overcome this?

Exercise #2 – Change It Up

Change feels weird. That's why we're so resistant to it so, today, make a change to your looks. **Wear an outfit that you wouldn't normally wear to work, change your hair parting, just mix things up. How did it feel?**

IN OTHER WORDS **DEFINED**

Why do you think we are so resistant to change in other situations?

How can you make it easier to accept change?

Exercise #3 – Transformational Words

In the space below, create a list of words that pop into your mind when you think of change. Don't think too long, just write what pops into your mind.

IN OTHER WORDS — DEFINED

Now that your list is complete, read it aloud and make a note of whether your response was negative or positive.

Why was that your response and how can you change it?

_____

Exercise #4 – As If

This is a visualization exercise. **Visualize yourself as being the successful person you want to be, the person who embraces change and makes it work to their advantage.** Imagine how you walk, talk, dress, think and interact with others. **Describe the person you visualized below.**

_____

IN OTHER WORDS > DEFINED

Now, what do you need to do to become that person? How can you dress, talk, act, think, and interact with others to get to where you want to be?

IN OTHER WORDS **DEFINED**

What are you waiting for? Be that person now!

MAP #9:
TRAVEL – Transforming Reality And Victoriously Exceeding Limits

MEANING
TRAVEL – Transforming Reality And Victoriously Exceeding Limits
I'm free to create my own reality

"You are the master of your destiny. You can influence, direct and control your own environment. You can make your life what you want it to be."
- Napoleon Hill

APPLY

Who does better in life, the internal victim or the master of their own destiny? When put that way, it's hard to choose the victim. However, using your victim status does grant you rewards and sympathies. It is also a valid reason why some things are harder for you than others. Something bad happened to you that was not your fault, but someone else's.

Embracing the role of the victim, however, prolongs your wounds and distracts you from taking control. You will cast yourself as the victim in situations where you are not, and you will often end up hurt again. Seek help for your pain, but do not identify as a victim. Instead, choose to create a different reality.

We all create our own realities, like it or not. All kinds of things happen to us, but our interpenetrations grant or steal our power. If you think you're a loser, you will not succeed because you think you don't deserve to. If you think you're a hard worker, you will spend the time and effort to make your dreams reality.

Changing your mind about yourself and reality takes time, but it starts with an intention. Intend to create a better self-image and life for yourself, even if you think it's impossible. Focus on that intention and make the changes you need to.

Sleeping more, eating better, and getting exercise are often simple changes that will revolutionize your outlook. If you find people intimidating, ease yourself into social situations. Talk to one new person a day, go to a work outing sometime.

Your fate is far from set in stone. You are who you think you are, so spend some time figuring out exactly who that is. Then, if the view doesn't serve you, discard it and create a better one! Transform your reality. Reach beyond your limits.

 **PROVOCATION – YOUR TURN**

Exercise #1 – Visualize the Next Level

One important aspect of exceeding limits is focus. A handy tool for remaining focused is visualization. You have to focus on your goals to maintain motivation so that you are capable of victoriously exceeding limits. You know where you've been, you know where you are, it's about where you want (or need) to go. **So, in the space below fully visualize the next level. This visualization should serve you daily, walk through it every morning when you wake up. Be as detailed as possible in your visualization – focus on engaging all of your senses to make it as real as possible.**

_____
_____
_____
_____
_____
_____
_____
_____
_____
_____
_____
_____
_____
_____
_____
_____

IN OTHER WORDS > DEFINED

Exercise #2 – Eliminate Weakness

Where weakness exists you will find your limits. We all have a series of strengths and weaknesses. Those weaknesses tend to subtract from our strengths. It's like springing a leak in a kayak. While it's important to focus on your strengths, it's equally as important to eliminate or manage your weaknesses.

WEAKNESS	SOLUTION

Exercise #3 – Embrace Larger Challenges

To exceed your limits, you first must embrace challenges that are more difficult than you're accustomed to. If you aren't regularly trying to exceed your limits, then you're going to experience paralysis in the comfort zone. You will stagnate and slip into despair.

Take a look at your day and the challenges you frequently face. How can you push yourself further outside of your comfort zone to embrace larger challenges?

IN OTHER WORDS DEFINED

Exercise #4 – Push Your Limits

While it's important to transform reality and exceed limits, it has to be deeper than just that. This isn't about pushing your limits just to challenge yourself. It isn't to prove you're courageous enough to do it. It's about growth. It's about testing your limits to move you forward and closer to your passion and purpose. **Stop looking at limits as a challenge to overcome and start framing them as an opportunity to grow.**

RESTRICTIVE LIMIT	HOW TO EXCEED IT

IN OTHER WORDS DEFINED

MAP #10:
VACUUM – Vision And Creation Under Unusual Makings

MEANING

VACUUM – Vision And Creation Under Unusual Makings
I am creating the life of my dreams

"When you believe in your dream and your vision, then it begins to attract its own resources. No one was born to be a failure." - MYLES MUNROE

APPLY

Life is an art. If your life has not been easy, you might find this statement cheesy. It's true, though. A hard life is a work of art and you are the artist behind it all. Is it the one you wanted?

You may not believe it, but you have the power to create the life of your dreams. If you disagree, try to name an advantage that thinking yourself powerless would give you? What we believe is often true. Those who believe they can change their life make changes and stay positive.

Those who think it's useless to try don't try and feel bitter. It is your choice to make, of course, but if you are unhappy with your life, I urge you to embrace this idea: you have the power to create the life of your dreams.

First, to achieve your dreams you must have a vision. You might be stuck on something vague like wanting to be happy. That's an amazing goal, but do you know what kind of life would make you happy?

You might also be stuck on something superficial. Do you want the trouble of maintaining a mansion? Do you love guitar enough to play it for a living? Maybe you do! If, however, you don't… that's also great! You can cross those dreams off and find better ones.

Once you have decided what kind of life you want, write down some short term and long term goals. Make sure they are achievable so that you don't set yourself up for failure.

By **YSIDRA RIVERS**

Your first goal may be as simple as going to bed an hour earlier so that you aren't exhausted all day. Then, once you've achieved a few goals, go back to your lists and evaluate them. Do you still want the same things?

Adjust accordingly and create that dream life you deserve!

 **PROVOCATION – YOUR TURN**

Exercise #1 – Know Your Desires

This is step one – you have to know what you want. How can you achieve it if you can't even describe it? Use the space below to create a record of what you want. This should be fairly easy if you already have a dream or a goal in mind. If you don't, clear your mind and freely write about things you love so much you completely lose track of time when you do them.

_____
_____
_____
_____
_____
_____
_____
_____
_____
_____
_____

IN OTHER WORDS — DEFINED

Exercise #2 – Know Your Why

When you know what you want, you have to figure out why you want that. So, in the space below, write about why you want to do it.

IN OTHER WORDS DEFINED

Now, write out your mission statement using the information from above.

IN OTHER WORDS **DEFINED**

_____
_____
_____
_____
_____
_____
_____
_____
_____
_____

Exercise #3 – Know Your Schedule

It isn't real if it isn't featured on your calendar. Above, you wrote about what you want, why you want that, and your mission statement. It's time to figure out how you're going to get there. **To do that, you need to schedule the action you are required to take. So, grab your diary or calendar and plan!**

Exercise #4 – Protect the Schedule

If this really matters, then you are going to do exactly what you have said you will do. That means you're going to have to protect the schedule you just created on your calendar. You're going to run into fear, you will experience doubt and uncertainty. You have to give yourself permission to protect your schedule and put yourself first. **How am I going to protect my schedule? Write a promise to yourself that you will do whatever it takes to stick to your promises.**

_____
_____
_____
_____

IN OTHER WORDS — DEFINED

MAP #11:
WICH – Who's In Charge Here

MEANING
WICH – Who's In Charge Here
I have the power to change myself

"Take charge of your life! The tides do not command the ship. The sailor does." - Ogwo David Emenike

"Your journey is completely yours. It is unique. Others may try to steal part of it, tell it in their words or shape it to suit them. Reality is, no one can live it or own it but you. Take charge of your journey, it's yours and yours alone!"
- Kemi Sogunle

APPLY

Some believe that destiny is preset, and they have little control. But there are those who strongly believe that they have full control over their thoughts, actions, life and ultimately their destiny. The later are usually the most fulfilled and successful.

By relinquishing your control to some idea of destiny, you also get out of taking responsibility for your decisions, choices and life.

Take charge of your life!

By **YSIDRA RIVERS**

When you build a mindset of control, you can then make plans for your life, and take full responsibility for how it turns out.

You can decide who you want to be. You can control your thoughts, your actions and begin to manifest the destiny you yourself decide.

There are so many things in life over which we have control: your mind, your decisions, your choices, your path, your thoughts and feelings, just to name a few. Ultimately you have full control of yourself!

When you realize and accept that you have full control over yourself and your life, you understand that your destiny is very much within your control. You can overcome the obstacles that stand in your way, one of the biggest of which is you.

Can you remember a time when your body was acting like an immature rebellious child? You had every intention of taking action. Your mind was screaming, go, go, go! But you could not make a move. You might consider this rebellion, but perhaps it was procrastination. There are times in our life when we must be honest with ourselves and ask questions.

At these times, when our bodies refuse to obey what our minds dictate, we must ask ourselves, "Who's In Charge Here?"

When you ask the question, answer the question and immediately take action.

 **PROVOCATION YOUR TURN**

Exercise #1 – Practice Confidence

Confidence is necessary to take charge in any situation, even if it's only yourself you're battling. This is your opportunity to set a challenge that will help you grow in confidence.

What are some of your biggest fears?

_____
_____
_____
_____
_____
_____
_____

What can you do to smash them and move forward?

IN OTHER WORDS — DEFINED

What situations make you feel most confident?

_____
_____
_____
_____
_____
_____
_____
_____
_____
_____
_____
_____
_____
_____
_____
_____
_____
_____
_____
_____

How can you capture that confidence and practice it in other situations?

_____
_____
_____
_____
_____
_____

IN OTHER WORDS DEFINED

_____
_____
_____
_____
_____
_____
_____

Exercise #2 – Stand Smarter

To truly take charge, you need to be confident, hold yourself in high esteem and feel smart enough to take charge. How can you do that? Well, spend time with people who are smarter than you, it forces you to up your game.

The five smartest people I know are…

1.

2.

3.

4.

5.

The five activities I can do to increase my knowledge are…

1.

2.

3.

4.

5.

Exercise #3 – Stretch Your Social Muscles

We often lose grip on control and who's in charge when we join a social situation. Often, social groups have an unspoken hierarchy and it doesn't matter what you do, as soon as you step into that group it kicks in. While you could be the boss at work, the moment a certain friend appears you're suddenly the butt of every joke. You don't have to stand for that.

Seek out a social event and strike up a conversation with a stranger. How did it go?

_____
_____
_____
_____
_____
_____
_____
_____
_____
_____
_____
_____

IN OTHER WORDS DEFINED

Have a conversation with someone you know holds different beliefs to you. How did it go?

You don't have to be in control everywhere you go, but you don't have to let others put you in a position you're not comfortable with either. If there's one thing you do have control over, it's you.

Exercise #4 – Challenging Situations

If you want to hold the control and be the boss of your own destiny, then you have to put yourself in situations where that isn't the case at all. How can you be the boss if you struggle to remain calm when you're the slightest bit uncomfortable?

Five situations that make me feel uncomfortable...

1.

2.

3.

4.

5.

How I can manage these situations more appropriately and remain calm...

1. _____
_____
_____
_____
_____
_____
_____
_____

2.

3.

4.

IN OTHER WORDS DEFINED

5.

MAP #12:
WIDE – Write It Down Exactly

 **MEANING**
WIDE – Write It Down Exactly
Today I take a step toward my dreams

"The great majority of people are "wandering generalities" rather than "meaningful specifics." The fact is that you can't hit a target that you can't see. If you don't know where you are going, you will probably end up somewhere else. You have to have goals." - Zig Ziglar

"By recording your dreams and goals on paper, you set in motion the process of becoming the person you most want to be. Put your future in good hands—your own." —Mark Victor Hansen

 **APPLY**

WIDE has been one of my most effective self-affirmations I've created. It's one I use more often than any other one.

Write It Down Exactly! Not only is there power in your spoken words, there's also power in your written words. Writing requires a single minded focus. When we are writing something, we view it to be important. When we write, it is with intent and we use thoughts and emotions from both our mind and our hearts.

Writing down our goals has the same effect as verbal affirmations. Just as your outer ear needs to hear what your inner voice is saying, your eyes need to see completely and clearly what the mind has created.

By **YSIDRA RIVERS**

IN OTHER WORDS DEFINED

Journaling and writing help you process your thoughts, emotions. It is a great way to organize both feelings and thoughts in a way where you can gain insight, understanding and direction. This is especially true in the very busy and hectic modern world, where quiet time to just think and process is hard to find. For those who have difficulty with focus, and being organized in mind, writing helps to make much more sense of what is going on inside of you.

Daily journaling is a great way to monitor and progress toward your goals. A journal allows you to explore your ambitions and therefore provides you with the much needed clarity to achieve your goals.

A journal is also the perfect vessel to brainstorm obstacles and problems and identify solutions. Writing a detailed plan for your goals greatly increases the probability of success. Writing also keeps those goals at the forefront of your mind so you are much more likely to take action to further success.

By **YSIDRA RIVERS**

Through writing we enhance our creativity, and this has many benefits for mind, body and spirit. Research has found creativity to improve brain function and actually stimulates different areas of the brain than other activities.

Perhaps one of the greatest benefits of writing is that it allows us to self-reflect. Self-reflection is key for personal growth and overall wellness, and it can help you discover so much about yourself.

Manifestation is the art of making what you want to happen through vision, action and intent. Writing your desires is one of the key practices in manifestation. It makes your desires real; it makes them solid. Write exactly what you desire and exactly what you desire will manifest!

 **PROVOCATION YOUR TURN**

Exercise #1 – Be Specific

A goal should be well defined and clear. There is nothing helpful about a vague goal. Keeping your goals general means you aren't providing yourself with enough direction. It's an easy way out. **Your goals should be your guiding light, bear that in mind as you write three specific goals below.**

1. _____

_____

_____

IN OTHER WORDS ▶ **DEFINED**

2. _____
_____
_____
_____

3. _____
_____
_____
_____

Exercise #2 – Make it Measurable

A goal should always include dates and measures. You can't keep track of your progress if you can't measure what you're doing. For example, you can't say you want to simply save money without defining how much money you will save and how often. **Take the three goals from above and write them in a way that is measurable.**

1. _____
_____
_____
_____
_____
_____
_____
_____
_____
_____

IN OTHER WORDS DEFINED

2.

3.

IN OTHER WORDS — DEFINED

Exercise #3 – Keep Goals Attainable

Are your three goals attainable? While it's detrimental to growth to set easy goals, it's equally as dangerous to set goals you cannot accomplish. **Look at the three goals you chose, do they meet the standard? How can you write them to ensure that they do?**

1.

IN OTHER WORDS — DEFINED

2.

3.

Exercise #4 – Goals Should Be Relevant

Are the goals you have written relevant to your values, beliefs, and the ultimate direction for your life? You will struggle to achieve things that don't align with who you are. **How can you write your goals to highlight their relevance to your greater self?**

1.

IN OTHER WORDS DEFINED

1.

2.

3.

IN OTHER WORDS | DEFINED

Exercise #5 – Time Bound

Finally, the goal has to have a deadline. A deadline helps create a sense of urgency. It makes it more real. **Create a timeline for the goals you have recorded above.**

1.

IN OTHER WORDS DEFINED

2.

3.

IN OTHER WORDS — DEFINED

The final step is to put it all together in a final action plan where you highlight how it all fits together.

My Goal	Specific	Measurable	Attainable	Relevant	Time Bound

MAP #13:
FILM – Faith In Live Motion

MEANING
FILM – Faith In Live Motion
I trust in the process of life

"Feel the present, hold the vision. Let go of the resistance, enjoy the journey And trust the process" - Frederk Talloen

APPLY

Faith is believing in something that has not yet occurred, usually this means something intangible. True faith does not waiver, it is something that remains through doubts and without reservation. This takes a lot of trust, but faith in essence is trust in something you cannot see or something that has not yet occurred.

Faith promotes positivity, helps you focus on what needs to be done, and is quite comforting as the surrender you feel yields peace of mind. It is a positive mindset that promotes patience and prompts you to act.

Faith is not hoping for something that you have. Faith is doing! Faith is an action. Faith is the doorway in which our expectancy flows out and the entrance to receive that which we hope for.

Jim Rohn articulated faith in its simplest form. "Faith is the ability to see what does not yet exist."

FILM is experiencing, in your right now, in your action, what has not yet manifested!

Faith In Live Motion is giving life to that vision that lies in the deepest of yourself. Seeing it more fuller today than you did yesterday, seeing it even greater tomorrow.

Faith In Live Motion is preparing yourself constantly, with ceaseless thoughts and conversations that are consistent with both your preparation and thoughts about what you believe you have; what you're experiencing from what you've created. And being grateful for it all.

 **PROVOCATION – YOUR TURN**

Exercise #1 – Affirmations

This is your opportunity to create affirmations that align your intentions and energy. You can make them up for yourself or you can do a quick online search to find a few affirmations you feel fit best. They don't need to associate to a specific goal, it can simply be about your overall energy and alignment. **Regardless of how you create those affirmations, record five of them below.**

1.

2.

3.

4.

5.

Now scribble them down on sticky notes and places them in spots you will see them regularly. Repeat them often.

Exercise #2 – Gratitude Journal

This exercise is one you can return to often. You don't need a physical journal, grab a piece of paper to scribble on or a notepad. **Each night before bed, starting tonight, write three things that you're grateful for.**

1.

2.

3.

Don't stop there – you have to ask yourself how those things tie into your intentions and goals. It's all about maintaining your intention and making your visions a reality.

Exercise #3 – Why Five Times

Enlist a helper for this exercise. Have them ask you one (or all) of the following questions.

- What do you deeply care about?
- What do you deeply desire?
- What do you truly want?

Answer quickly, as soon as an answer pops into your mind just blurt it out. Your helper should then tease more information from you with follow up questions.

- Why do you want it?
- If you achieved it, what would you have?

Again, you should respond quickly with the first answer that comes to you. The helper should repeat that final question multiple times and you should answer with whatever comes up each time.

Do you have a greater sense of your vision now?

Exercise #4 – A Higher Version of Yourself

Calling on a higher version of yourself means taking that vision you've held of yourself and turning it into a reality. It's about acting it, knowing it, breathing it, sleeping it... how does it feel, how does it act, what does it talk and look like? This is something you should grow. As you call on this version of yourself, the world will help reflect it back on you.

Describe this higher version of yourself. What is your vision?

_____
_____
_____
_____
_____
_____
_____
_____
_____
_____
_____
_____
_____
_____
_____
_____
_____
_____
_____
_____
_____
_____

IN OTHER WORDS DEFINED

IN OTHER WORDS > DEFINED

MAP #14:
GRAPH – God Respects A Pure Heart

 **MEANING**
GRAPH – God Respects A Pure Heart
My words and actions reflect my heart and soul

"At the end of the day, I am at peace because my intentions are good and my heart is pure."- Anonyms

"A pure heart won't get us out of conflict and controversy. It may be the very thing that gets us into it." - John Hagee

 **APPLY**

Webster's Dictionary defines pure as: "unmixed with any other matter."

Our heart represents more than just an organ in our physical body, our heart is the center of who and what we are. Our center, that place from which we are anchored, where our core values are created and sustained, and the place we can easily go within. Our heart.

Our heart is our home. It is familiar. Comforting! Fulfilling! Familiar! It is our shelter when the world grows cold. The heart is where we find ourselves.

Home is a place where you can always, always, always return to. When the storms rage! When health is challenged! When we need to recuperate, refuel and refresh. When we just want to enjoy peace. Sometimes, we don't have a reason.

IN OTHER WORDS — DEFINED

Home is where the heart is, and our heart is a place we call home! A safe place. A trusted place. An honorable place. A secure place. A place worth protecting. A place well guarded.

When our heart is well and at peace, so are we and our lives. A peaceful heart means we are living in peace and free of major conflict.

Webster's Dictionary defines Respect as:

a. high or special regard
b. b: the quality or state of being esteemed

God Respects A Pure Heart. Our efforts to guard, honor, protect and secure our hearts so that no other matter enters in, is esteemed by God even if and when we're not able to guard it thoroughly, protect it totally and secure it completely.

By **YSIDRA RIVERS**

 **PROVOCATION YOUR TURN**

Exercise #1 – Identify Values

It's difficult to ensure your words and actions reflect what you believe within yourself if you haven't first identified your values. Let's do that now. **If you were to describe your greatest experience – what values were on show and what were you doing?**

_____
_____
_____
_____
_____
_____
_____
_____
_____
_____
_____
_____
_____
_____
_____
_____
_____
_____
_____
_____
_____
_____
_____
_____
_____

IN OTHER WORDS — DEFINED

If you were to describe your worst experience – what values were suppressed and what was happening?

IN OTHER WORDS / DEFINED

IN OTHER WORDS DEFINED

What fundamentals do you make your significant decisions based on?

IN OTHER WORDS DEFINED

When you die, how would you like to be remembered?

IN OTHER WORDS DEFINED

To make your life unbearable, what would need to be taken away?

IN OTHER WORDS DEFINED

_____
_____
_____
_____
_____
_____
_____
_____
_____
_____
_____
_____
_____
_____

Look at the answers you have given and pick out themes that will help you determine your core values. The values you feel are crucial to life and happiness.

Exercise #2 – Work Values

While many of us would prefer to work to live rather than the opposite, the work we do can conflict with our values. It's difficult to maintain a pure heart and protect ourselves when the work we do goes against our values. You can't just walk away from your job so, it's vital that you look at the job you do and find the ways in which it *does* align with your values. Focus on that so that you can maintain a pure heart while looking for work elsewhere or changing your life to reflect your inner self.

Does your company invest resources in good deeds?

_____
_____
_____

IN OTHER WORDS ⟩ DEFINED

What key values does your firm hold?

_____

_____

_____

What tasks do you complete that align with your values?

_____

_____

_____

_____

_____

_____

_____

_____

_____

_____

_____

_____

_____

_____

Exercise #3 – Make an Action Plan

This isn't just any action plan; this is an action plan to encourage you to practice your values at all times. **You can create an action plan for any value disconnects, as well as actions you can take to live and speak your values.**

VALUE	WORK	HOME	SOCIAL LIFE	DISCONNECT

Exercise #4 – Cleaning up Your Language

The words you use drive your actions; they drive your thoughts. It's time to clean up your language. So, instead of saying *but* say *and*. Drop *should* from your language and replace it with *want to* and *because*. Forget *I'm going to* and stick with *I am*. For example:

Sure, you have a point, but I can totally see Mario's point **VS** Sure, you have a point, and I can also see Mario's point.

I should call my client Jeremiah **VS** I am going to call my client Jeremiah because I want to clinch this sale.

I am going to launch my business with David this year **VS** I am launching my business with David.

Now, take sentences you commonly use and rewrite them like the above examples. Complete three for each example.

1. _____
2. _____
3. _____

1. _____
2. _____
3. _____

IN OTHER WORDS DEFINED

1. _____
2. _____
3. _____

MAP #15:
No PMS – No Poverty Mind Sets

MEANING

No PMS – No Poverty Mind Sets
Being successful is my natural state

"Mindset is what separate the best from the rest." - John Assaraf

"When you master your mindset, you free yourself to achieve the level of success you desire." - Frederique Murphy

APPLY

No PMS! No Poverty Mind Set! I think about Abram, from the story in the Book of Genesis where Abram knew nothing of God. God established a relationship directly with Abram; thus, Abram is considered to be the father of faith.

Abram believed in something that he could not see. Abram followed the instructions of God, who was not tangible. Abram left everything that he knew and everything that he had. I believed that God called Abram to do that because of the mindset of his family.

No PMS! Poverty does not only apply to money. We can be impoverished in our minds. We can be impoverished in our health. We can be impoverished in our relationships. We can be impoverished in our language.

IN OTHER WORDS DEFINED

Adopt a No Poverty Mind Set! We have the power to create. It is written, there is nothing impossible for God.

The opposite of an impoverished mindset is the abundance mindset, which believes that all is possible and there are plenty of success resources to go around. An abundance mindset sees a bright and optimistic world where accomplishments are ready for the taking.

The abundance mindset views failures as opportunities.

The abundance mindset is proactive and takes the necessary positive steps toward success and avoids harmful situations.

The abundance mindset is optimistic and positive.

By **YSIDRA RIVERS**

The abundance mindset longs to manifest dreams, goals and desires and takes actions in furtherance of such goals.

The abundance mindset is wealthy and rich.

No PMS! When one continues to live in their past, they're living an impoverished life. Why live in your past when you can have a very very bright future? A future that you can create for yourself.

No Poverty Mind Set! We all have a purpose! We all have desires! We all have dreams! Most of us have actually created vision boards. Most of us have visualized having/building our own business.

We must be absolutely positively confidently prepared and assured that poverty is not a part of our mind set.

We must be sure to not hang with or spend must time with or take counsel from those with limited thoughts, limited language and impoverished thinking.

We must be ever so careful not to take on the likeness of anyone that lives in an impoverished state. No Poverty Mind Set!

PROVOCATION – YOUR TURN

Exercise #1 – Mind Map

A visual exercise will help you gain control over your mindset by highlighting your goals and interests. Use the space below to create your own. At the center, write the current year. Now, draw spokes coming from it and label them with the different areas or themes of your life that you value. Think social life, career, romance, fitness, fun, health, and growth. Each of these themes should have its own spokes detailing how you'd like to improve that area. Dream big and be prepared to fight hard.

_____
_____
_____
_____
_____
_____
_____
_____
_____
_____
_____
_____
_____
_____
_____
_____
_____
_____

IN OTHER WORDS — DEFINED

Exercise #2 – Challenge Your Current Mindset

Use the table below to question the thought. We have provided an example to get you started, from there you should use your own experiences to complete the table.

THOUGHT	QUESTION	ACTION
I just can't do this, it's beyond me. If I try, I'll just fail so, what's the point?	What strategy could I take to approach this?	I can apply the lesson I learned from failing to ensure I succeed next time.

IN OTHER WORDS DEFINED

By **YSIDRA RIVERS**

Exercise #3 – Grow Your Grit

In this exercise, you will need to seek out a partner. This person should be someone you know has overcome great challenges in their life. Ask them the series of questions below and make notes on their answers.

What is the biggest goal you have set for yourself and managed to achieve?

_____
_____
_____
_____
_____
_____
_____
_____
_____
_____
_____
_____
_____
_____
_____
_____
_____
_____
_____
_____
_____
_____
_____
_____

What did you have to do to ensure you achieved this goal?

Did you ever consider giving up? What did you do when you felt like that?

How did it feel to finally accomplish this goal?

Exercise #4 – Grow Your Grit, Part 2

In part two, it's your turn. Answer the above questions for yourself.

What is the biggest goal you have set for yourself and managed to achieve?

___

IN OTHER WORDS ▶ **DEFINED**

What did you have to do to ensure you achieved this goal?

IN OTHER WORDS **DEFINED**

Did you ever consider giving up? What did you do when you felt like that?

IN OTHER WORDS DEFINED

How did it feel to finally accomplish this goal?

MAP #16:
SYSTEM – Save Your Self
To Escape Mediocre

 **MEANING**
SYSTEM – Save Your Self To Escape Mediocre
I embrace opportunities that can make a positive change in my life

"Step out of the crowd of average people. Enter that game and change the values on the scoreboard." — Israelmore Ayivor

 **APPLY**

The dictionary defines mediocre as: "of only moderate quality; not very good."

SELF, you are not mediocre!

Yes, you may see it in the marketplace, in the media and sometimes in the magazine, you may even see it in your mother.

SELF, do not allow mediocre to be your model. Escape Mediocre: of only moderate quality, not very good!

Adopt SYSTEM!

System is defined as a set of procedures according to which something is done, an organized scheme or method. SELF, you were not created to live a boxed life. You are too creative, too powerful and frankly to damn amazing to be of mediocre quality.

Your life quality hinges for the most part on how you feel about yourself. If you feel mediocre you will act mediocre and cease to seek all the best in life that you deserve.

Learning to love yourself fully and completely is the first step in creating the best possible life and self that you can be.

Everything stems from our self-esteem, how we treat ourselves, the people we attract into our lives, our mindset and the goals we choose for ourselves.

One of the best ways to develop and maintain a positive relationship with yourself is to start learning to love yourself. Increasing your self-esteem will help you realize what your strengths and weaknesses are and will make you feel comfortable in your own skin.

Boosting your self-esteem begins with a conscious decision to love yourself, take good care of yourself and be kinder to yourself.

With high self-esteem we will no longer feel mediocre.

SELF, not only are you good, but when you were created, it is written that you were VERY GOOD!

Adopt SYSTEM! Do not become a part of the mediocre mindset! Save Your Self (for yourself) To Escape Mediocre!

 **PROVOCATION YOUR TURN**

Exercise #1 – Just Say Yes

How often do you pass up opportunities because you're too scared to seize the day? **Use the table below to think about some chances you have passed up, how it could have changed your life, and what you will do the next time a similar opportunity arises.**

IN OTHER WORDS DEFINED

OPPORTUNITY	POTENTIAL POSITIVE CHANGES	HOW WILL I RESPOND IN THE FUTURE?

Exercise #2 – Create a Snowball

Don't allow the world to overwhelm you, create a snowball effect by making small changes to create larger changes. **You have made goals throughout this workbook. Take one of those goals and in the space provided below, create a series of steps to contribute to your snowball.**

Exercise #3 – Define Yourself

It's vital that you define yourself and find a role model who models success. If you look up to someone who is mediocre, then you yourself will be mediocre.

Define yourself as you are now.

_____
_____
_____
_____
_____
_____
_____
_____
_____
_____
_____
_____
_____
_____
_____
_____
_____
_____
_____
_____
_____
_____
_____

IN OTHER WORDS DEFINED

Define your role model.

IN OTHER WORDS **DEFINED**

Define yourself as you would like to be following in the footsteps of your role model.

Exercise #4 – Enhancing Your Self-Image

It's time to take a two minute self-image break. In the space below, write about what you appreciate. More specifically, what you appreciate about you.

_____
_____
_____
_____
_____
_____
_____
_____
_____
_____
_____
_____
_____
_____
_____
_____
_____
_____
_____
_____
_____
_____
_____
_____
_____
_____

IN OTHER WORDS DEFINED

MAP #17:
TEACH – Taking Empowerment Above Common Horizons

MEANING
TEACH – Taking Empowerment Above Common Horizons
Everything is possible

"You must decide if you are going to rob the world or bless it with the rich, valuable, potent, untapped resources locked away within you"
- MYLES MONROE

"Those who know, do. Those that understand, teach." - Aristotle

APPLY

Today will be the best day of the rest of your life.

How is that? Why is that? With your gratefulness and the power of it and that which manifest from it.

Today you will create your own door to open. Today you will not wait for a place to be given to you, you will take your own place. Today you will go towards people with confidence and bring your own power into their space and when you leave, you will leave them EMPOWERED!

When you can realize and accept how powerful you really are, you will have power over yourself and your life. Powerlessness often occurs because we don't realize our own power, or we give it away to other people, places or things. A lack of confidence is often a reason we don't embrace our personal power and instead we trust others to make decisions for us rather than being true to ourselves.

Personal power is inner strength. Personal power is control of self. Possessing, owning and using your own personal power makes you empowered.

Personal power is all about mastering yourself. It involves knowing yourself and being willing to learn more every day. It also means being comfortable with yourself and being your true self in all situations.

In empowerment you embrace your own personal power, which includes accepting all parts of yourself, the good and bad and facing all the fears that are controlling you and stopping you from living your ultimate dream life or from being your true self.

Personal power means not being a victim of life or circumstance. It means knowing what you want from your life and taking full responsibility for your life and your actions.

When we are empowered, we don't blame others or life for our negative situations, instead we go and make the necessary changes to improve these and to strive forward. No one can give you personal power; it is something you find within yourself and this makes you self-empowered.

 **PROVOCATION YOUR TURN**

Exercise #1 – New Ideas

Today, I want you to sell a new idea. It could be a chore chart at home or a new process at work. Whatever it is, it's up to you to come up with the idea (it doesn't have to be big), figure out how to pitch it and get everyone's buy in to implement it.

THE BIG IDEA	THE PITCH	THE BUYIN & IMPLEMENTATION

Exercise #2 – Self-Assessment

What do you possess that no one else does? What is one thing you can do for others that no one else can do or is prepared to do?

UNIQUE SKILLS	SUPPORTING TRAITS	HOW I CAN USE THIS TO EMPOWER MYSELF

Exercise #3 – Flex Your Assertiveness

To empower yourself you must learn to assert yourself. In what ways can you assert yourself today?

ASSERTIVE ACT	EMPOWERMENT

Exercise #4 – Empowerment Through Delegation

The best way for some to learn is by doing. So, you can empower others by delegating tasks and placing your trust in them to complete them as required. **Today, you're going to delegate a series of tasks to people in your life and trust in them to take care of business.**

TASK DELEGATED	PERSON DEALING WITH TASK	OUTCOME

MAP #18:
AFTER – Allowance For The Emergency Room

MEANING
AFTER – Allowance For The Emergency Room
I take time for renewal

"It's better to be prepared for an opportunity and not have one, than to have an opportunity and not be prepared." — Les Brown

"When you prepare for something big in your life and work towards it with such intensity, it takes confidence to take a day off and have peace with it."
J.R. Rim

"If you're proactive, you focus on preparing. If you're reactive, you end up focusing on repairing." — John C. Maxwell

APPLY

After you have given to your spouse! After you have given to your children! After you have given to your employer! After you have given to your clients/customers! After you have given to your parents! After you have given of yourself, all of yourself you've had to give, there must be a ready place to give to yourself to refuel, refresh and refine you!

This place must be prepared, in advance. It must be as a reservoir.

Sometimes even after you've given the best of yourself to your spouse, children, employer, clients/customers and to your parents, what you gave is still not enough for them.

Sometimes they will not say thank! Sometimes they will not be grateful! Sometimes they will expect more than you have to give. Sometimes knowing all you had was not enough can be discouraging.

AFTER you have given all of yourself to all those you serve, in any capacity, there must be Allowance For The Emergency Room and tell yourself I SEE YOU (ICU)!

 **PROVOCATION – YOUR TURN**

Exercise #1 – Schedule

Do you have a to-do list? Join the club. There's a good chance other people feature heavily on your list, but do you? It's time to revisit your schedule. **Cross off anything that doesn't *need* to be done and make that time for you.** Read, watch a movie, take a nap, and heal thyself. How did it feel to take time for yourself to practice self-care?

IN OTHER WORDS ▸ DEFINED

Exercise #2 – Moisturize

The act of applying moisturizer to your skin is more meditative than you realize. You aren't just feeding your skin; you're feeding your soul. **Grab a bottle of your favorite lotion and slowly apply it to your hands, arms, feet, and legs. Allow yourself to fully focus on this act alone. How did it feel?**

_____
_____
_____
_____
_____
_____
_____
_____
_____
_____
_____
_____
_____
_____
_____
_____
_____
_____
_____
_____
_____
_____
_____
_____
_____
_____

Exercise #3 – A Mini Meditation

One form of mini meditation is to name your emotions. By naming them you become more aware of them and remove their power. Let's try it now.

Detail a negative experience you had today.

_____
_____
_____
_____
_____
_____
_____
_____
_____
_____
_____
_____
_____
_____
_____
_____
_____
_____
_____
_____
_____
_____
_____
_____

IN OTHER WORDS / DEFINED

What words would you use to describe the emotions you went through during this experience?

_____
_____
_____
_____
_____
_____
_____
_____
_____
_____
_____
_____
_____
_____
_____
_____
_____
_____
_____
_____

Detail a positive experience you had today.

_____
_____
_____
_____
_____
_____
_____
_____

IN OTHER WORDS / DEFINED

What words would you use to describe the emotions you went through during this experience?

Did you notice a shift in your brain and thinking as you completed this task?

Exercise #4 – Journal to Relieve Stress

There is power in journaling. It allows you to get things off your chess and let all of your stress out on a page. **While I recommend you invest in a nice notebook for a permanent journal, there is space below to get you started.**

_____
_____
_____
_____
_____
_____
_____
_____
_____
_____
_____
_____
_____
_____
_____
_____
_____
_____
_____
_____
_____
_____
_____
_____
_____

IN OTHER WORDS DEFINED

MAP #19:
RARE – Releasing A Radical Expectancy

 **MEANING**
RARE – Releasing A Radical Expectancy
My outlook on life is infused with enthusiasm

"The true alchemists do not change lead into gold; they change the world into words." - William H. Gass

"Waking up to who you are requires letting go of who you imagine yourself to be." - Alan Watts

"Imagine going through a door, this great barrier. When you get in and look back from the other side, you find out that there is no door." - Alan Watts

 **APPLY**

Did you know that there are 3 aspects of ourselves?

1) The aspect which we know we know (i.e. we know our names)
2) The aspect which we know we don't know (i.e. we know we don't know how to build a rocket)
3) The aspect which we don't know what we don't know

Let's make a decision to do a rare thing monthly!

The aspect which we don't know what we don't know is in a dimension we rarely go! For instance, when we are in a certain state (mentally, spiritually and emotionally simultaneously) there are certain laws that are working to the degree of which our state exists.

When we are in a state of gratitude (mentally), secure (not resisting) and we make a decision or have a purpose, things are set in motion to accomplish whatsoever that decision or purposed thing is.

Today, RELEASE A RADICAL EXPECTANCY to be accomplished FOR OURSELVES!

 **PROVOCATION – YOUR TURN**

Exercise #1 – Strengths & Weaknesses

It's important to know both your strengths and your weaknesses. **What are your top five strengths?**

1.

2.

3.

4.

5.

What are your top five weaknesses?

1.

2.

3.

4.

5.

Exercise #2 – Self-Reflective Questions

What attitude do I have toward myself?

___
___
___
___
___
___
___
___
___
___
___
___
___
___
___
___
___
___
___
___
___
___
___
___
___
___
___
___

What attitude do I have toward others?

Are my thoughts and actions positive?

IN OTHER WORDS / DEFINED

Do I show tolerance and consideration for others?

Do I genuinely respect the opinions and rights of others?

Do I often interrupt others while they speak?

IN OTHER WORDS — DEFINED

Am I being honest with myself?

Do I act arrogantly?

Am I persistent without being aggressive?

Do I stick to my beliefs or do I jump from opinion to opinion?

Do I build habits that make me a better person?

Am I confident in my abilities?

Exercise #3 – Self-Reflective Journal Prompts

Use these prompts in your journal

- If I could choose to spend my day in any way, it would be...

- If I could give advice to my former self, the one thing I'd advise is...

- The most unforgettable moment of my life was (describe in detail) ...

- 10 things that make me smile/laugh.

- Three words I live by are...

- I can't imagine my life without...

- The kindest thing I can do for myself when I am in emotional or physical pain is...

- The 3 people who support me most are...

- To me, unconditional love means...

- If there is one thing, I wish everyone could know about me it's...

Exercise #4 – Write a Bucket List

List 10 things you would love to do before the end of the year.

1.

2.

3.

4.

5.

6.

7.

8.

9.

10.

Now, list another 10 things you'd like to complete before you die.

1.

2.

3.

4.

5.

6.

7.

8.

9.

10.

MAP #20:
BEG – Being Exceedingly Grateful

M **MEANING**
BEG – Being Exceedingly Grateful
I experience gratitude daily
The more grateful I am the more reasons I find to be grateful

"Gratitude is the attitude that takes you to your altitude." - Anonymous,

"Do not spoil what you have by desiring what you have not. Remember that what you now have was once among the things you only hoped for" - Epicurus,

"Be thankful for what you have; you'll end up having more. If you concentrate on what you don't have, you will never, ever have enough." - Oprah Winfrey

 **APPLY**

Gratitude carries that same amount of substance as a hardy laugh. Have you ever laughed so hard that tears came to your eyes? That same substance within you, in that moment, is the same substance, in the same measure, as when your heart is filled with gratitude.

Gratitude is highly effective in boosting our emotional, mental and physical health. It is also one of the most effective ways to improve your life quality. Gratitude is a hallmark of a positive mindset and optimism, where no matter how bad things might get in life and even when you are facing stress, difficulties and struggle, you see the silver lining and are able to maintain peace of mind and peace of heart.

Gratitude brings benefits for everyone, including those with anxiety and depression.

When we focus on appreciating all we have we are better able to cope with life on life's terms and respond to negative emotions in healthier ways. Research finds that the regular practice of gratitude activates parts of the brain linked to compassion, empathy and positive mood.

Furthermore, practicing and expressing gratitude allows us to be more fulfilled, promotes happiness and improves self-esteem. Need more? Gratitude also improves optimism, furthers progress towards achieving goals, increases determination, supports healthy sleep and even helps alleviate light aches and pains.

Being Exceedingly Grateful brings about a sense of wholeness. To BEG is a choice!

BEG is an unearthly state. It's as if you are bringing heaven to earth. Be Exceedingly Grateful is so effective, that it heals emotions, it changes the waves in our brains, and it's also contagious.

Let's choose to BEG, daily!

 **PROVOCATION – YOUR TURN**

Exercise #1 – Attitude for Gratitude

Three things I'm grateful for…

1.

2.

3.

Three things I take for granted…

1.

2.

3.

Exercise #2 – Self-Gratitude

Three things I appreciate about myself...

1.

2.

3.

Three things I'm grateful for in my life right now...

1.

2.

3.

Exercise #3 – Social Gratitude

Three people I am grateful for who have had a positive/significant impact on my life...

1.

2.

3.

Now, write a thank you letter to these three people. You don't have to send them, and it doesn't have to be a long letter.

1.

2.

3.

Exercise #4 – The One Thing

Using the lists, you created above, choose the one thing you are most grateful for. Allow yourself the time to meditate on it and appreciate it deep within your heart.

What did you choose?

_____
_____
_____
_____
_____
_____
_____
_____
_____
_____
_____
_____
_____
_____

What are your thoughts and feelings about it?

MAP #21:
BIOS – Belief In One's Self

M **MEANING**
BIOS – Belief In One's Self
I follow my instincts

"The strongest factor for success is self-esteem: Believing you do it, believing you deserve it and believing you'll get it." - Anonymous,

"When you believe in yourself, you have 100% of the people you need on your side." - Anima Vitam

"A bird sitting on a tree is never afraid of the branch breaking, because her trust is not on the branch but on its own wings. Always believe in yourself." - Les Brown

A **APPLY**

Belief in self is key in achieving anything in life, and to live your best life and be your best self. The most critical aspect of the drive to succeed is a strong, unwavering belief in self. Confidence greatly fuels your belief in self.

Self-management and self-discipline are keys in staying on track with your belief in yourself and achieving all that you strive for. Doubts are common and powerful, we all doubt ourselves at one point or another, BUT belief is more powerful than doubt, so reach for it, revel in it and keep it at the forefront of your mind.

There should be nothing more important to you than your BIO! You must know what makes up your BIO, what your BIO consists of. Without a deep, solid, strong BIO, there can be no confidence in serving or giving to others. There is a sense of boldness that grows within us when self-belief is developed.

Belief In One's Self is detrimental to our journey. Without a belief in self we are crippled in striving for goals, with living well and ultimately gaining complete and total satisfaction over our lives and ourselves. Self-belief means we are confident, self-assured and know we are capable to do anything we set our mind to.

BIOS comes with a certain attitude which is required on our journey. The wrong attitude could take you off course, create unnecessary detours and delays and attract the wrong people into our lives.

 **PROVOCATION – YOUR TURN**

Exercise #1 – Love Yourself

Ten attributes I love about myself...

1.

2.

3.

4.

5.

6.

7.

8.

9.

10.

Exercise #2 – I Have Skills

Ten skills I possess...

1.

2.

3.

4.

5.

6.

7.

8.

9.

10.

Exercise #3 – I Can Achieve

My ten biggest achievements...

1.

2.

3.

4.

5.

6.

7.

8.

9.

10.

Exercise #4 – I Can Overcome

Five challenges I have overcome…

1.

2.

3.

4.

5.

Exercise #5 – I Can Help

Five people I have helped in overcoming their challenges…

1.

2.

3.

4.

5.

MAP #22:
BOWS – Be Okay With Silence

 **MEANING**
BOWS – Be Okay With Silence
My spiritual quest brings me fulfillment

"The quieter you become the more you are able to hear." - Rumi

*"The monotony and solitude of a quiet life stimulates the creative mind."
- Albert Einstein*

"Silence isn't empty, it's full of answers." - Unknown

 **APPLY**

Noise is everywhere! Both wanted and unwanted! Can you imagine how obese we would be if our weight was affected by the amount of noise we heard? The unfortunate thing is that we have become immune to the noise.

Just as there is external noise, we also have our own internal noise. That chatter within is a repeat of the noise we've unconsciously recorded from one time or another. We have unchecked thoughts replaying, conversations rehearsing and maybe a few voice messages, text, tweets that we need to respond to.

Often, during conversations we have with others there exists an uneasiness during long pauses. It's almost as if the mind of each person that is a part of the conversation is racing and desperately searching for something to say to break the silence.

Silence is a beautiful thing. Silence clears and calms the mind. Silence makes us centered. In silence we can find answers to our deepest felt questions. In silence, we find our truest selves. In silence, we hear ourselves clearly and profoundly.

Embracing silence can be likened to a detox. And just like a detox, silence takes time. You may not be comfortable with a total state of silence right away or even quickly, but the process of learning to be in silence is worth the discomfort and the frustration.

The modern world is loud. Be Ok With Silence, not matter how it comes, when it comes, where it comes or how often it comes. Seek it out. Practice it. Live it. It Is Ok!

PROVOCATION – YOUR TURN

Exercise #1 – Inhale, Exhale Colors

There is no greater activity for silence than a breathing exercise. In this exercise, you will visualize colors.

Choose a color that you view as relaxing, one that makes you feel at ease.

_____

Now choose a color that represents anger, stress or sadness.

_____

As you inhale through your nose, imagine the air you breathe being the relaxing color you chose. As you exhale through your mouth, imagine the air you expel being the stressful color you chose. This is something you can do anywhere.

How did it make you feel?

Exercise #2 – The Body Scan

One of the keys to embracing silence is focusing solely on something else. In this case, a body scan. Sit or lay comfortably. Bring your focus to your feet for ten seconds. Move that focus slowly to your toes, then your ankles, calves, knees, gradually scanning every area of your body until you reach the top of your head. When you reach an area of stress or tightness, you should breathe through it imagining that you are exhaling the stress away.

How did each of your body parts feel?

Did they feel hot or cold?

Did they feel relaxed or tight?

Exercise #3 – Breathing Hands

Spread your dominant hand like a star. With your other hand, outline your star hand with your index finger. Breathe deeply as touch your thumb, exhale as you move to the index finger, inhale again at you reach the index finger, and so on.

You can get a bit of quiet even amidst chaos. **This exercise is about growing comfortable with silence. How did it make you feel?**

Exercise #4 – In The Still of the Night

If there is something that represents your emotions best, it's your heartbeat. It's always with you, just like your breath. One way to grow comfortable with silence is by tuning into your heartbeat. It allows you to connect with the moment when you're dealing with stress or feeling uncomfortable with silence.

Begin this exercise by taking three deep breaths. Place your hand or fingers on your wrist or neck, wherever you can best feel your pulse. We'll call this the heartbeat position.

Close your eyes and tune into your heartbeat. Is your heart beating slowly or quickly?

IN OTHER WORDS — DEFINED

How does this fit with your current emotional state?

Now, do ten jumping jacks and return to the heartbeat position. Can you notice a change?

www.ingramcontent.com/pod-product-compliance
Lightning Source LLC
Chambersburg PA
CBHW080730230426

43665CB00020B/2686